+

09√

D1411984

Medieval Castles

© Aladdin Books Ltd 2007

Designed and produced by
Aladdin Books Ltd

Printed in the United States

All rights reserved

First published in the United
States in 2007 by

Stargazer Books
c/o The Creative Company
123 South Broad Street
P.O. Box 227
Mankato, Minnesota 56002

Library of Congress Cataloging-in-
Publication Data

Adams, Brian.
   Medieval castles / by Brian Adams.
      p. cm. – (Hallmarks of history)
   Includes index.
   ISBN: 978-1-59604-119-6
   1. Castles--Juvenile literature.
   2. Civilization, Medieval--Juvenile
   literature. I. Title. II. Series.

GT3550.A33 2006
940.1--dc22
                          2005055541

Revised edition published in 2007.
Original edition published as History Highlights – Medieval Castles
Author: Brian Adams
Back cover   A 15th-century drawing of the castle in Saumur, France
Design: David West Children's Book Design
Editor: Harriet Brown
Illustrator: Rob Shone
Map: Aziz Khan

Contents

HALLMARKS OF HISTORY

Medieval Castles

Stargazer Books

Introduction

Castles can be found all over Europe. Some are romantic ruins while others are grim reminders of the violent Medieval or Middle Ages. Medieval castles were built to protect those who lived in or near them from their enemies. The castles had walls built around them. People lived in buildings within the walls.

The Normans (from Normandy, France) invaded England in 1066. The Saxons (who had settled in England earlier) hated their new masters for seizing their land, so they attacked the Normans. To establish their rule, the Normans built a network of castles. They were often built at river crossings, mountain passes, or other important places.

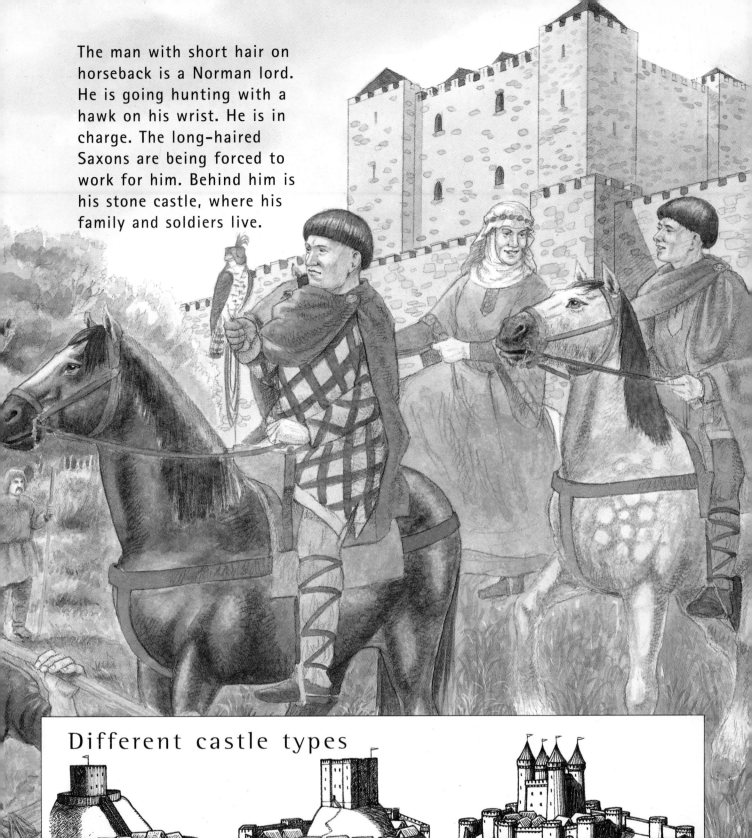

The man with short hair on horseback is a Norman lord. He is going hunting with a hawk on his wrist. He is in charge. The long-haired Saxons are being forced to work for him. Behind him is his stone castle, where his family and soldiers live.

Different castle types

At first the Normans had wooden castles. They built a tower on a mound of earth (called a motte) with an open area round it (a bailey).

Later castles were made of stone. They had a large stone tower or keep as well as a bailey. The walls were of stone with square towers.

Eventually, larger rooms were built within much stronger walls. Castles with two sets of walls were called concentric.

Fighting and defenses

Castles had strong walls to resist attack from an enemy. As castles became larger, more than one set of walls were built. Beyond the walls there was a ditch or a moat. Moats were filled with water which soldiers found difficult to swim across. However, it was easy to build a raft and float across the moat. So dry ditches were dug, which made it hard for the attackers to get close to the walls.

The men defending the castle would fire arrows or stones at the attackers. If the attackers reached the walls, they would use long ladders to climb over them. The defenders used long forked poles to push the ladders off. If the wall was taken, the defenders would move into the wall towers and fight from there.

Gateways

Wall towers had heavy wooden doors which were closed and barred when an attack began. Another defense was a portcullis. This was a heavy wooden and iron grating with spikes at the bottom. To close it, the portcullis was lowered on chains. The chains were wrapped around a large wooden roller turned by a wheel. It was very heavy so the men working the portcullis had to be strong. The portcullis was part of the main gatehouse, which was heavily guarded.

Attackers also used wooden siege towers. They had huge wheels so they could be moved up to the walls. The defenders would hurl garbage or boiling water at them. Later castles had holes in the walls through which water or boiling oil could be dropped.

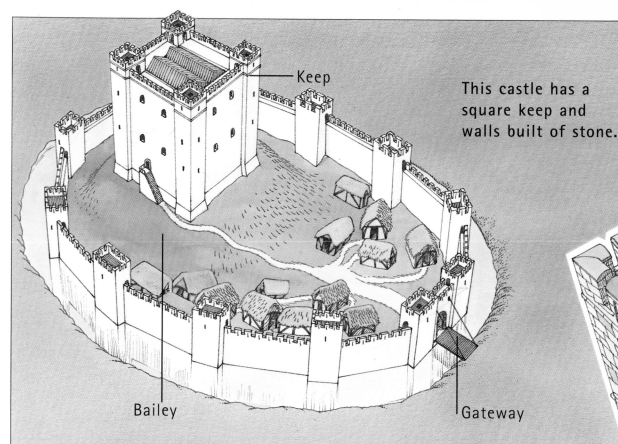

Keep

This castle has a square keep and walls built of stone.

Bailey

Gateway

Inside the keep

The large square keeps of the 12th century housed soldiers as well as the lord of the castle and his family. The main room was the Great Hall where everybody ate. The lord sat on a raised platform. Above the hall was the private room where he and his wife lived. The soldiers lived below the hall. This was a noisy area that also contained the kitchens.

Castle supplies were stored in the basement. Prisoners were either made to work around the castle or kept in smaller rooms upstairs. They were held until someone paid for their release.

Each floor had at least one large fireplace. Smoke escaped through special holes in the walls. The walls were almost ten feet (three m) thick in some castles.

The staircase for the keep was built so that the defenders had the advantage. They could use their swords freely while the attackers could never really see their enemy.

8

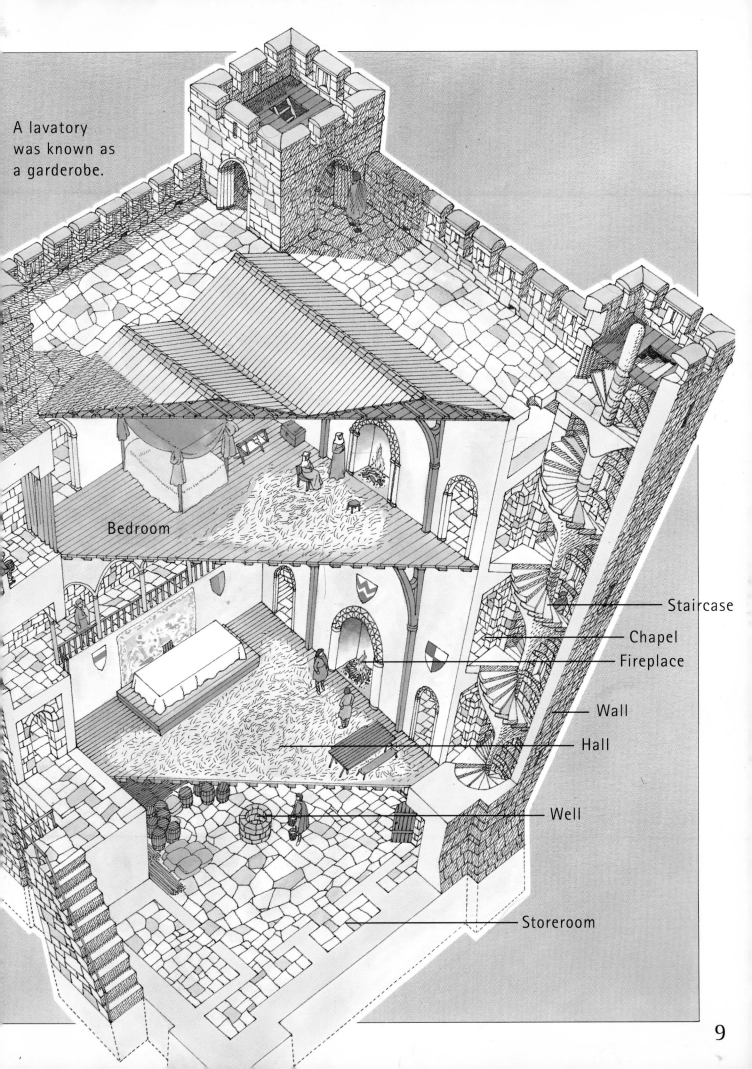

A lavatory was known as a garderobe.

Bedroom

Staircase

Chapel

Fireplace

Wall

Hall

Well

Storeroom

Queen Eleanor

Private rooms in castles had wall hangings and tapestries. Furniture was plain, but was covered with rich material. Lords took furniture with them from one castle to another.

Eleanor of Aquitaine was married to the English king, Henry II. She was a lively and intelligent woman, who owned much land in France. Henry wanted to control her lands. Queen Eleanor plotted against Henry with her sons. Henry won and kept her as a prisoner until he died in 1189. Then her son Richard, who had become king of England, released her.

The queen is shown in her private room. Henry kept her in great comfort. Here she is playing a game similar to the modern game of checkers. The pieces are made from walrus ivory.

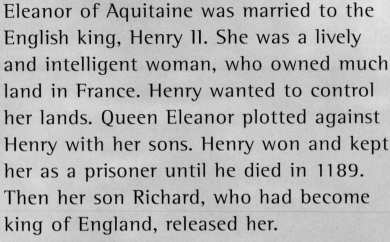

King

Barons and church

Knights

Cottars

Villeins

Serfs

The feudal system

Kings and queens were able to rule their countries by giving land to their followers in return for their services and taxes. Land was passed down the feudal system. Everyone owed loyalty to the one who gave them land. The serfs had no land and were bound by law to their lords.

Castle people

A medieval castle housed the lord and his family, his soldiers, and the servants who looked after them.

There was a lot of work involved in running a castle. Blacksmiths or armorers were very important. They had to shoe horses, repair tools, and look after the soldiers' armor. The soldiers patrolled the countryside on horses, which had to be looked after in stables. Carpenters made furniture and repaired carts. Others looked after the buildings. There was usually a plumber to make new pipes and lead roofs.

Life in the Middle Ages was hard. People did not live as long as they do today—many died of diseases, like the plague, and others died in wars. A 40-year-old was considered old.

Cooking in a castle

This is the kitchen at Glastonbury Abbey. Sometimes kitchens were built in the bailey. Several men worked in the kitchens preparing food. Food was obtained from the surrounding countryside. During a siege, people had to survive on animals living within the bailey or on salted or dried food. Some castles had their own fishponds and dovecots. They provided fresh food throughout the year.

Growing up in a castle

Children ran errands and delivered messages. However, very few ever went to school. Bright boys would be taught by monks at a nearby monastery. Girls were taught how to cook and sew by their mothers. Rich families paid a teacher to educate their children. In poorer families, sons were trained by their fathers to do a job or craft.

Sons of noblemen were taught how to become soldiers and leaders in battle. Some boys were sent to live in a nobleman's house to learn leadership. They were called squires. Part of their training involved looking after their lord's armor, holding his horse for him to mount, or carrying his food to him.

This covered wagon carried women and young children on long journeys. It had no springs, so it must have been uncomfortable to travel in. Most adults went on horseback if possible.

Toys and games

Boys played sports similar to modern-day soccer. They also rode hobby horses. Girls had wooden dolls. Children also enjoyed "hoodman blind" where someone was blindfolded and tried to grab the other players.

Building Château Gaillard

Château Gaillard was built in France on a cliff overlooking the Seine River. Château means castle in French. Gaillard was built by Richard I of England in the 1190s. He put it there to protect his lands in France from attack. The castle was divided into sections. Each section had to be captured before the castle could be taken.

Gaillard was a new type of castle and looked very hard to attack. Even so, it was captured by the French king, Philip Augustus, in 1204. The French got inside the castle after a soldier climbed up a lavatory chute. He let the rest of the army in by opening one of the windows. Shortly afterward the English had to surrender.

Richard I saw to the building of Château Gaillard himself. It was built quickly. Carpenters, masons, and plumbers came from all over Normandy. Good timber and building stone from the area were carried using horse-drawn wagons.

Date chart

1189 Richard Coeur de Lion becomes King of England.

1195 Richard has to give his castle at Gisors to the French king, Philip Augustus. Decides to replace it with a new castle at Les Andelys near Rouen.

1197–98 Château Gaillard is built very quickly.

1199 King Richard is killed at Chalus by a crossbow arrow. John becomes King of England.

1203 Philip Augustus begins siege of Château Gaillard with a huge army. The French build banks and ditches around the castle.

1204 The French attack begins. The French finally capture Château Gaillard. This was an unusually long siege for a medieval castle. Town sieges could last a lot longer.

1215 Philip Augustus adds strong towers to outer walls.

1300 Importance of Château Gaillard at an end. It is neglected and becomes a ruin.

Today the ruins of Château Gaillard are a national monument and have been heavily restored. They can be visited on the banks of the Seine River, in France.

Castle sieges

Castles were built to resist sieges. Sieges were not always successful but they could go on for a long time. A siege usually only lasted a few weeks but in 1224 one lasted for three months. After that time, the food in the castle ran out and those inside had to surrender.

It was not always easy for the attackers. They had to camp in tents outside the walls until the castle surrendered. Sometimes, other armies would attack them and drive them off.

Those under attack would try to unnerve the enemy. They would throw bread off the walls to show that food was still plentiful. They also used dummies to make it seem that there were more soldiers inside than there really were.

Siege equipment

Stone walls could be smashed with battering rams or climbed using a siege tower. Bits of wood were thrown into the ditch to fill it so that the tower could be pushed right up to the walls. Walls were attacked with stones or fireballs. They were fired from a mangonel. This had a large timber piece shaped like a huge spoon. It was held down by ropes. When the ropes were released, the timber shot up and fired the missile.

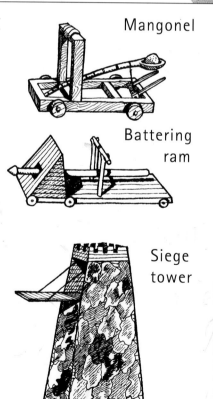

Mangonel

Battering ram

Siege tower

A tunnel would be built under the wall. The tunnel was supported by timber. This would be set on fire. The tunnel would then collapse bringing part of the wall down.

19

Saumur Castle

This beautiful castle looks over the French town of Saumur. It was built by the Duc d'Anjou at the end of the 14th century. A lot of money was spent on the building. There were gilded weathercocks, bell turrets, and fine carved stonework. Around Saumur there are vineyards. Even today the area is famous for its fine wines.

Later castles

After 1350, castles were no longer used just for defense. People wanted to live in greater comfort so new buildings were put up, sometimes within castle walls. There was a new way of building, known as Gothic. Gothic windows had pointed arches and were much larger. They let in more light.

Toward the end of the Middle Ages, some castles became very grand. They looked like fairy tale castles with pointed roofs and brightly painted walls. Stone carvings were put on arches, windows, and walls. Rich people became interested in gardens, planting roses and other flowers.

The people are waiting to see the lord of the castle. The man on the right is wearing a long-sleeved gown and a hat based on Arab headgear. His wife has a hat with a net to tie in her hair.

21

Tournaments

The men taking part in a joust wore helmets with their crest or badge on top, so that everyone could tell who was fighting whom.

A tournament was a great occasion, which often went on for days. It was held outside the castle and attracted many visitors. The main event was the joust. Two men would charge each other on horseback. Both wore armor and their horses were covered in embroidered cloth. The men held long blunt wooden lances and would try to knock each other down. They did not try to kill each other, but usually ended up badly bruised. There were archery competitions, wrestling matches, and sword fights at a tournament.

Tournaments began in France in about 1050. Jousting tournaments were ideal for men to practice fighting and prove their skill.

The age of chivalry

You could succeed in life if you followed the rules of chivalry. Honor and fair play were taken very seriously. Men would write poems to the women they loved and try to win their love. If a man loved someone else's woman, one way to settle the argument was to take part in a tournament.

Feasts

At times, food was scarce for everybody, not just the poor. Bread was the basic food. The wealthy used thick slices of brown bread as plates to eat on. They were called trenchers. Fish was the second most common food. Chickens, ducks, or geese were popular foods. On special occasions the better off ate swan and peacock. Beef and venison were well liked, and pigs were kept for pork.

Vegetables were grown in the castle gardens. Herbs were used to season food or make remedies when people fell ill. During the Middle Ages, new foods, like raisins, dates, and figs, were brought to Europe by the Crusaders. Spices were very expensive because they came all the way from the Far East.

Most people used their fingers to eat their food. Forks were brought in toward the end of the Middle Ages. Many people thought that using forks was silly. There were many rules on the correct way to eat and where people had to sit at the table.

Eating

This is a reconstructed medieval kitchen at Cotehele in Devon, England. Food was cooked in metal pots called cauldrons. Meat was roasted on large spits over a fire.

Since glass was too expensive, food was stored in pots or wooden barrels. The rich had bowls made of pewter or even cups of silver and gold. Plates were rarely used.

Bowl

Goblet

Knife

Wooden board

What happened to castles?

As the Middle Ages came to an end, strongly defended castles became out-of-date. A few shots from a cannon could easily knock a wall down. This was shown very clearly during 17th century wars. In central Europe the Thirty Years' War began in 1618, while in England the Civil War began in 1642. Both wars were very bloody and caused terrible damage.

In England, Oliver Cromwell's army was well organized. The soldiers had modern armor and very powerful cannons. But it was not always easy to capture large castles. Such castles had many towers and enormously thick walls. Pembroke Castle in Wales was attacked by Cromwell himself in 1648. The siege lasted from May 22 to July 11.

Cromwell's army attacks one of King Charles I's castles during the English Civil War. If the castles were too expensive to repair, they were abandoned. Only castles that were still used by the army, like Dover, were kept in good condition.

New designs

Tilbury Fort was built in the 15th century. In the 17th century, it had new walls built. They were very thick to withstand cannon fire. The walls stuck out so that the defender's cannons had a clear firing area.

Castles worldwide

Castles are found throughout the world. Ch'ang-an in China was a huge rectangle over 5 miles (8.5km) wide and almost 5 miles (8km) from north to south. It was built in the 7th and 8th centuries by the T'ang emperors. Ch'ang-an was as large as Baghdad in Iraq, which was probably the largest city in the Middle Ages.

The Moscow Kremlin, in the former Soviet Union, has 19 towers and pink colored walls almost 66 feet (20m) high. It was built in the 15th century for the Russian Czars.

Further west, in Germany and Poland, castles were built by powerful men called the Teutonic Knights. In other parts of Germany and Switzerland important men also built castles.

Japanese castles

This is Himeji castle in Japan. Castles there were built mainly of stone. They were quite simple buildings. After the 16th century they had thick, high walls. Because of earthquakes in Japan, the walls curved inward and were strengthened. This was to stand up to the shock of the earthquake.

This impressive site is in southern Africa. The ruins are called the Great Zimbabwe. They were built after 1200. The stone walls were beautifully made.

Date charts

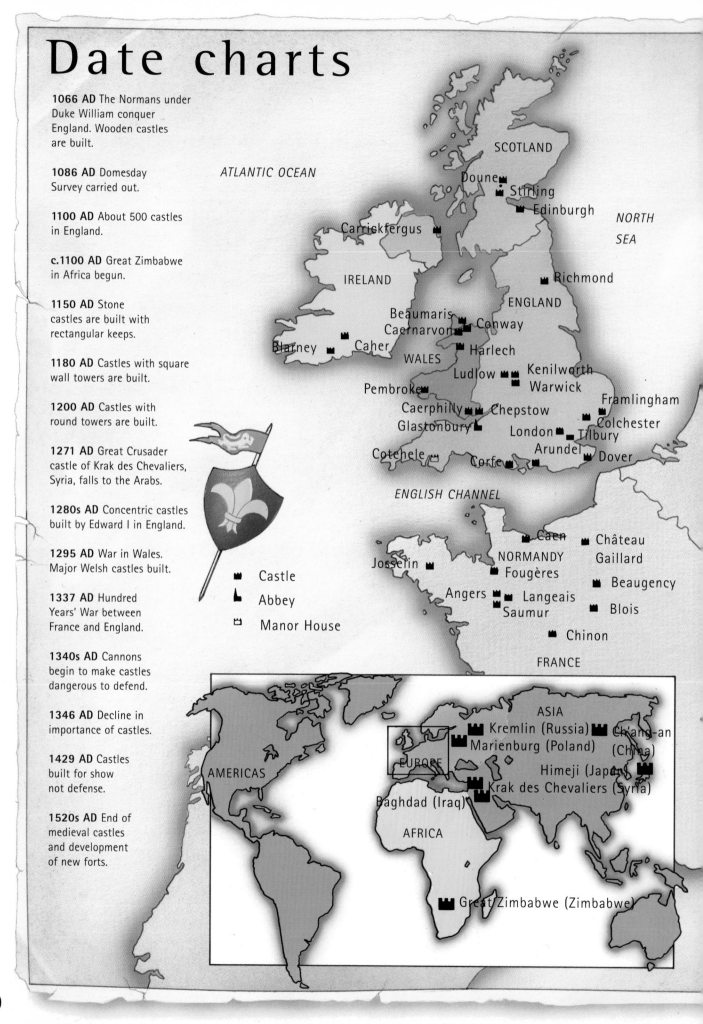

1066 AD The Normans under Duke William conquer England. Wooden castles are built.

1086 AD Domesday Survey carried out.

1100 AD About 500 castles in England.

c.1100 AD Great Zimbabwe in Africa begun.

1150 AD Stone castles are built with rectangular keeps.

1180 AD Castles with square wall towers are built.

1200 AD Castles with round towers are built.

1271 AD Great Crusader castle of Krak des Chevaliers, Syria, falls to the Arabs.

1280s AD Concentric castles built by Edward I in England.

1295 AD War in Wales. Major Welsh castles built.

1337 AD Hundred Years' War between France and England.

1340s AD Cannons begin to make castles dangerous to defend.

1346 AD Decline in importance of castles.

1429 AD Castles built for show not defense.

1520s AD End of medieval castles and development of new forts.

ATLANTIC OCEAN

SCOTLAND

Doune

Stirling

Edinburgh

NORTH SEA

Carrickfergus

Richmond

IRELAND

ENGLAND

Beaumaris

Caernarvon

Conway

Blarney

Caher

Harlech

WALES

Ludlow

Kenilworth

Warwick

Pembroke

Framlingham

Caerphilly

Chepstow

Colchester

Glastonbury

London

Tilbury

Cotehele

Arundel

Dover

Corfe

ENGLISH CHANNEL

Caen

Château Gaillard

Josselin

NORMANDY

Fougères

Beaugency

Angers

Langeais

Blois

Saumur

Chinon

FRANCE

■ Castle
▲ Abbey
♜ Manor House

AMERICAS

EUROPE

ASIA

Kremlin (Russia)

Ch'ang-an (China)

Marienburg (Poland)

Himeji (Japan)

Krak des Chevaliers (Syria)

Baghdad (Iraq)

AFRICA

Great Zimbabwe (Zimbabwe)

Africa	Asia	Americas	Europe
641 AD Arabs take over Egypt and overrun North Africa.	**618 AD** Establishment of T'ang Dynasty in China.	**500 AD** Beginning of Mayan civilization in central America. Development of Teotihuacan.	By **500 AD** Roman Empire in Western Europe has collapsed and is overrun by barbarians.
700 AD Arab traders set up trading settlements in East Africa.	**751 AD** Arabs defeat Chinese in central Asia.		
800 AD The kingdom of ancient Ghana trading across to the Sudan.	**907 AD** End of T'ang Dynasty.		**800 AD** Charlemagne crowned emperor in the West. Vikings from Scandinavia attack British Isles.
	960 AD Sung Dynasty in China.		**911 AD** Vikings settle in Normandy.
	c.1000 AD Gunpowder in China.	**980 AD** Toltec capital set up at Tula (Mexico).	
			1066 AD Norman conquest of England.
1054 AD Ghana conquered by Almoravid Berbers.			**1096 AD** First Crusade.
c.1100 AD Beginning of the building of the Great Zimbabwe.		**1151 AD** Fall of Toltec Empire.	
c.1235 AD Sun Diata Keita establishes the Kingdom of Mali.	**1210 AD** Mongols invade China under Genghis Khan.		
	1279 AD Sung Dynasty falls to the Mongols.		**1295 AD** First representative parliament in England.
c.1300 AD The Empire of Benin in Nigeria emerges.			**1314 AD** Poland is reunited following Mongol raids.
	1368 AD Ming Dynasty in China takes over from the Yuan Dynasty.	**1350 AD** Beginning of Aztec Empire, becoming independent after 1428.	**1348 AD** Bubonic Plague sweeps across Europe.
1400 AD Decline of Zimbabwe. Growth of state of Benin. In southern-central Africa Kingdom of Great Bantu develops.	**1421 AD** Peking (Beijing) becomes capital of China.	**1438 AD** Inca Empire in Peru expands.	**1415 AD** English victory over French at Agincourt, during Hundred Years' War.
		1450 AD Incas conquer Kingdom of Chimu.	**1429 AD** French begin reconquest of France.
			1500 AD End of Middle Ages.
	1526 AD Mogul Empire of India founded.	**1521 AD** Cortés conquers Tenochtitlàn.	
		1533 AD Pizarro brings down Inca Empire.	

Index

Photographic credits:
Pages 7, 13 and 20: The Ancient Art and Architecture Collection/Ronald Sheridan; page 17: Michael Holford; page 25: National Trust Picture Library; page 29: Hutchison Library; back cover: Bridgeman Art Library